BELONGINGS

Morgan Lloyd Malcolm

BELONGINGS

OBERON BOOKS
LONDON

WWW.OBERONBOOKS.COM

First published in 2011 by Oberon Books Ltd
521 Caledonian Road, London N7 9RH
Tel: +44 (0) 20 7607 3637 / Fax: +44 (0) 20 7607 3629
e-mail: info@oberonbooks.com
www.oberonbooks.com

Reprinted in 2012, 2015

A catalogue record for this book is available from the British
Library.

PB ISBN: 978-1-84943-225-2
E ISBN: 978-1-84943-333-4

Cover image © VikaValter

Printed and bound by Marston Book Services, Didcot.

Visit www.oberonbooks.com to read more about all our books
and to buy them. You will also find features, author interviews and
news of any author events, and you can sign up for e-newsletters
so that you're always first to hear about our new releases.

Thanks to Clare and Purni at the National Theatre Studio for the time and space to write a first draft.

Will, Greg and Ed at Hampstead Theatre for seeing its potential and taking a chance.
My wonderful director Maria for all the support and encouragement to believe in it. And our amazing cast Jo, Kirsty, Cal and Ian who worked so hard and brought these characters to such vivid life.

Thank you to the amazing production team in particular, Sophie, Sarah, David, Carolyn, Naomi, Ed, Cressie and Corinne.

Thank you to Georgina and Sarah at David Higham Associates for waiting so long to get my first play out!

This play is for my amazing friends and family who have never failed to back me up, support me, read drafts and mop up any tears. You all know who you are and I raise a drink to you at any excuse...

But in particular Nell, Marlon, Mum and Dad, you are my sunshine. And my beautiful husband, Steve, you are my shining star.

Characters

JIM

DEB

JO

SARKO

Belongings is the fourth production to be shown as part of the Hampstead Downstairs programme. This production of *Belongings* was first performed at Hampstead Theatre, London, on 19 May 2011.The production extended to Trafalgar Studios on 16 June 2011. The cast was as follows:

JIM	Ian Bailey
DEB	Joanna Horton
JO	Kirsty Bushell
SARKO	Calum Callaghan

Creative Team
Writer, Morgan Lloyd Malcolm
Director, Maria Aberg
Designer, Naomi Dawson
Lighting, David Holmes
Sound, Carolyn Downing
Production Manager, Ed Wilson
Company Stage Manager, Sarah Cowen
Assistant Director, Sophie Ivatts

A detached new build home in a cul-de-sac somewhere outside Chippenham. The kitchen. A room split in two by a sideboard that creates a dining area at one end, kitchen at the other. Evening. DEB looks around the room – though it is her home, it has changed. Suddenly a completely naked man stomps in. This is JIM. DEB is positioned so that JIM doesn't notice her at first. He goes to a cupboard and is looking for something. DEB is finding it hard not to laugh and doesn't quite know whether to say something. Eventually JIM turns and sees DEB. He yelps out in fright. When they speak it is with Chippenham accents.

JIM: FUCK!

He makes no attempt to cover his modesty.

JIM: Jesus H fuckin' christ Deb! You scared the livin' bejesus out of me you fuckin'! What the?! When d'you get back then? Fuck!

DEB: Just now.

JIM: I'd bloody hug you if I didn't have my nob out.

DEB: Yeh. About that dad…?

He grabs a tea towel and covers up.

JIM: What, your dad's gonads not good enough for you eh?

DEB: Er…

JIM: Fuckin' hell you're back!

DEB: Yeh I am.

JIM: I thought I was gonna pick you up?

DEB: Me too.

JIM: You never told me when though.

DEB: Yeh I did. But no matter. Honestly. Got the bus.

JIM: Got the fuckin' bus? Fucksake. Serve our country and got the bus. Sorry mate.

DEB: Honestly don't stress.

JIM: Well I knew it would be today or tomorrow or somethin' I just didn't know the exact time.

DEB: Seriously. Don't.

JIM: Well. Look atchoo. Jo's gonna be stoked. Seriously. She's been plannin' your return dinner for weeks.

DEB: I don't want a fuss.

JIM: Why not?! Almost two years you dickhead.

DEB: Make that a year and a half.

JIM: You say potato. Oh mate. Not spent proper time with you in ages. Nice of you to bless us with your presence this time.

DEB: Don't start. You know I needed a holiday. A proper one.

JIM: Yeh I know. Glad to be home then?

DEB: Yeh.

JIM: Well I am. I'm glad you're home. All the shit in the papers about. Well. I'm glad you're in one piece. It would have been a fucker if you'd lost a limb eh? Got burnt or summat?

DEB: Better than dyin' though eh?

JIM: Is it? Complete change of lifestyle. Complete change to the way you live.

DEB: Yeh well. I had mates that we lost so. Maybe a drink?

JIM: Yeh you don't wanna be talkin' about this now eh? But I mean – we'd have had to convert this place for you. Do you get money to do that from the army? Do they sort you out with kit if you're disabled in combat and that?

DEB: Yeh I guess. Can I have a drink?

JIM: Help yourself. I doubt they'd completely help you though. I bet most of the burden lays on the family don't it? We'd be the ones left moppin' you up eh?

DEB: Yeh well I'm fine in-I? Can we leave it? Do you want one too?

DEB has gone to the fridge and pulls out a couple of beers.

JIM: Go on then.

DEB: All changed.

JIM: What's that then?

DEB: This place.

JIM: Jo did a rejig. Better aint it?

DEB: Yeh.

JIM: 'cept the frogs. Fucking frogs everywhere. Jo loves her frogs.

DEB: Yeh I know.

JIM: Lick of paint. Scrubbed up alright.

DEB: What did you do with all mum's stuff then?

JIM: Who's that then?

DEB: Dad…

JIM: Yeh alright. Chucked it didenI?

DEB: Yeh.

JIM: Well I weren't gonna keep it was I? Erect a shrine? She aint dead.

DEB: She may as well be.

JIM: Yeh too right mate. 'If I never see her again' and all that.

DEB: Yeh. Jo alright is she?

JIM: Course she is. Life of riley that girl. Got it made.

DEB: Yeh you're really livin' the high life aintcha?

JIM: I aint heard her complainin'.

DEB: She's done a good job. Anyways. Would you mind puttin' some clothes on maybe?

JIM: I'd just had a shower see?

DEB: I don't want to know what you've been doin' thanks. What were you lookin' for?

JIM: Fags.

DEB: In the kitchen cupboard?

JIM: Jo's been hidin' them. Tryin' to get me to stop.

DEB: Is it working?

JIM: Is it fuck.

DEB gets a pack of fags out and offers him one.

DEB: Here y'are.

JIM: Hold that thought. I'll be back after I made meself decent.

DEB: Gonna take more than clothes to achieve that.

JIM: Cheeky bastard.

JIM leaves. DEB lights her fag and drinks her beer. She surveys the room. The sound of the front door opening and closing and then JO enters. She is a few years older than DEB. She is carrying shopping bags which she drops as soon as she sees DEB.

JO: Deb! Oh! Whendyou get in then? Whendyou arrive? Oh! C'mere!

She embraces DEB who awkwardly and stiffly reciprocates, still holding her fag and beer.

DEB: No worries. Just now didenI?

JO: What a massive surprise you sneak! Your dad didn't know when you'd be ready for pickup. We didn't know when to expect you. I'm sorry Deb.

DEB: Don't worry mate honestly. How are you?

JO: Oh I'm fine but what about you? Look at you! All tanned up. Been sunbathin' out there have you?

DEB: Can't really avoid it. Did quite a bit of my duties in my sports bra to be honest. It was over fifty degrees sometimes.

JO: No! How can you do anythin' in that kind of heat?

DEB: You acclimatise.

JO: You must have been drinkin' gallons of water a day.

DEB: Yeh.

JO: Your dad and I were only sayin' the other day about this hot spell we're havin' that it probably isn't half as hot as where you were and we were bloody right then weren't we? I think we were somethin' like twenty-five degrees or summink! And there we were – all sparked out on the patio. Didn't get nuffin' done. Twenty-five degrees and we're no use to anyone.

DEB: Yeh?

JO: Well you know your dad. Any excuse to just loll about. And then you're out there runnin' about in fifty degrees? You're like some action hero!

DEB: Yeh?

JO: Super-Deb!

DEB: Well.

JO: I got to get dinner goin' then!

DEB: I don't want a fuss Jo.

JO: Well tough tits you're gettin' one. A year and a half sweetheart. A year and a half. How long we got you for?

DEB: Don't know.

JO: Well how long's your leave?

DEB: I aint goin' back.

JO: Serious?

DEB: Yeh well. Done my time aint I?

JO: Yes you bloody have.

DEB: Yeh well.

JO: C'mere.

JO grabs her and hugs her. This time DEB is less awkward. She pulls away quickly though.

DEB: Alright calm down!

JO: Really pleased love.

DEB: Yeh I get it.

JO: I'm makin' lasagna! Where's your dad to?

DEB: He went to put some clothes on diden he?

JO: Well won't that make a nice change? Why don't you go and get out of your kit? Get yourself comfy and I'll get goin' with the food.

DEB: I want to stay down here and help you out.

JO: Well I want you to get settled back in. Relax.

DEB: Mate last time I saw you…

JO: Don't. Now you shush-up and if you aint goin' upstairs then you can help me lay the table or something. Make a change from our laps. I've got some candles somewhere. And I definitely have a lighter so. Right. Onwards. Let's get dinner on the go.

DEB: I like what you did. With this place.

JO: Yeh?

DEB: Different and that. But yeh. Made it yours.

Pause. Something passes between them. JIM enters and notices the quiet.

JIM: What, are we having a minute's silence in honour of the complete fuckin' lack of any dinner being cooked?!

JO: I'm on it.

JIM: My daughter's home and I wanna celebrate! C'mere!

He grabs DEB and bear hugs her and scrubs her head.

JIM: Well done for not gettin' yourself disabled!

DEB: Fuck off dad!

JIM: I'm already runnin' more websites than I can keep a handle on. More of a strain on the old resources and it would have got well tight.

DEB manages to extricate herself from his arms.

DEB: Still changing the world with your business ideas then?

JIM: You know me sweetcheeks. Gis that fag then. And don't fuckin' look at me like that Jo – I'm celebratin' the return of my daughter.

JO: I had my back to you Jim, I weren't lookin' anywhere near you.

JIM: Well I could feel you thinkin' it.

JO: Thinkin' what?

JIM: Thinkin' up new ways to make my life a misery.

JO: Well that's a nice way to speak to the woman who's makin' your dinner.

JIM: Well this is the man who's payin' for it. C'mon Deb – gis that fuckin' fag.

DEB, who has been hesitating as she listens to their conversation, takes a fag out of its packet and holds it out to JIM. However as she does the scene changes around her, JIM and JO disappear and…

SCENE 2

…We transition into the desert. The past.

Evening. DEB is still holding out her fag and SARKO enters, taking it from her. We're in the sleeping quarters. It's a big tent in which six soldiers are housed – sleeping on camp beds that can be made private by mini-tents around them. Their belongings hang in clothes tidies and sit in plastic boxes under their beds and posters adorn the walls – including several topless women. We only need see DEB and SARKO's beds. SARKO is holding a bottle of shower gel that has had a cock and balls drawn on it with a marker pen.

SARKO: Bored were you?

DEB: Someone got 'cocked'?

SARKO: Actin' all innocent.

DEB: What you lookin' at me for?

SARKO: 'Cos you were the one that done it a billion times before!

DEB: Don't lie!

SARKO grabs a plastic box of his stuff and holds up, one by one, his belongings that have been 'cocked'.

SARKO: Shampoo! Hair gel! Face cream!

DEB: Vain bastard. You've got more toiletries than me.

SARKO: Oh this is one I aint seen before. My toothbrush? You twat! My toothbrush?! That's just fuckin' wrong.

He demonstrates brushing his teeth with the cock facing front. DEB finds this hilarious.

DEB: I'm a fuckin' genius!

SARKO: I can't use this no more!

DEB: It's like you're sucking a nob!

SARKO: Yeh yeh. Laugh it up. So glad to know we've got you protecting our country.

DEB: Oh like you're so pure.

She holds up her hairbrush which has also been cocked and brushes her hair with it.

DEB: *(Playacting.)* Oh I wanted to brush my hair but someone keeps poking me with their hard-on.

SARKO: *(Laughing.)* Idiot.

Moment of calm as they settle. SARKO lights his fag.

SARKO: Cooled down a bit now aint it?

DEB: Yeh.

More fiddling with stuff. SARKO picks up a magazine. He sees that it has also been 'cocked'. He holds it up accusatorialy.

SARKO: Really?

DEB: You were fuckin' ages in the shower.

SARKO: Even Maggie? Beautiful pure Maggie?

DEB: Who?

He holds up a picture in the magazine of Maggie Gyllenhaal who has been 'cocked'.

DEB: Oh yeh, I know.

SARKO: Would you?

DEB: Who her? Yeh. Definitely. You?

SARKO: Nah. But I tell you who I would…

He flicks through the magazine.

SARKO: There's my girl – Charlize Theron?

DEB: Let's have a look? Not for me, no.

SARKO: Really? Lindsay Lohan?

DEB: No. Do you know why? She'd be too eager to please.

SARKO: That's a good thing aint it?

DEB: No it aint. Complete turn off. Eager to please equals low self-confidence. No thanks. I don't want someone giving me the porn star routine. All pantin' and 'ooohing'. I want genuine reactions. Give me Maggie any day. I reckon she'd be awesome.

SARKO: Not enough tits for me.

DEB: Why, how many do you want?

SARKO: Yeh yeh.

DEB: It's not all about the tits.

SARKO: It is for me.

DEB: Not that I don't like a nice pair; it's just not all about them.

SARKO: Ah bless you Deb. You old romantic.

DEB: Oh whatever.

SARKO: No it's lovely.

DEB: Dick.

SARKO: Need a bit of romance in this place eh? Need a bit of loveliness. This sandy. This sandy old. Pit. Of.

Pause.

DEB: You done then?

Pause. SARKO is thinking.

SARKO: I've got this theory about the desert.

DEB: Oh here we go…

SARKO: It's a place, right. That is stripped down to the very basics of life. There's fuckin' barely anythin' here. There's nothin'.

DEB: Right…

SARKO: It's a barren wasteland of nothing-ness. Hot, arrid, parched, neglected.

DEB: Yeh…

SARKO: Bit like your bush.

DEB: Fuck off!

SARKO: But anything here of any use to us is man-made. But still – there's not quite nothin' is there?

DEB: You just said there's nothing here.

SARKO: Shuttup. Because you still get shrubs. Or trees dotted about. Still there are the odd signs of life.

DEB: Where are you going with this?

SARKO: And my eyes aren't interested in the man-made stuff. It's the bits of life that catch me. Because more often than not they're hiding something or someone that wants to kill me. In a place so empty of life; the only bits of it there are can potentially kill. I'm including humans in this too by the way. We're fuckin' killin' each other in a place where life is fuckin' rare. It doesn't make sense. We should be holdin' on to whatever there is. We're an endangered species in the desert that's what we are.

A pause.

DEB: That's not a theory.

SARKO: What?

DEB: That's an observation you thick twat.

SARKO: What the…? Shut the fuck up I'm just tryin' to raise the fuckin' tone here.

DEB: You're what?

SARKO: Have an intelligent conversation. Get a bit fuckin' philosophical alright? Who are you? The pedantic fairy? Fuck off.

DEB: Easy up there Sark. Just puttin' my two pennies worth in.

SARKO: Well have it back. Next time I want a conversation I'll talk to that sandbag over there shall I? I'll get more respect from it.

DEB: Don't start a conversation like that if you don't want a response Sarko. Just because I disagree with you doesn't mean I don't want to talk about it. It's called a 'debate'.

SARKO: I know what it's called you patronising dick.

DEB: Oh look at you gettin' all puffed up like some rooster on steroids. Little prick – what's the problem?

SARKO: You are. Do you realise how high above the rest of us you place yourself? Notice that I said 'place yourself' because no one else has put you there. Just because you've made it out here with us it don't mean you're the queen of the fuckin' desert.

DEB: Ok you're ravin' now.

SARKO: You're still only a soldier like the rest of us. A bunch of fuckin' reject idiots who had nothin' better to do with our lives that give them up for a fuckin' country who barely even knows we're out here. Barely even knows it.

DEB: Where the hell did that come from?! Is that what you actually think?

SARKO: Fuck off.

DEB: We're the best army in the world mate. You know that. We're the best. I'm proud of being part of it. I always wanted to be a soldier. I'm proud to be here and I'm glad I'm 'only' a soldier like the rest of us. And I'm gonna work my way up that ladder until I'm fuckin' Major if I can.

SARKO: I don't know what we're doin' here is all.

DEB: Do you care? It's our job mate. And in my opinion we do it bloody well.

SARKO: Just sayin'.

DEB: Just sayin' what? Hot air. This place is gettin' to you is all. Why'd you go and put a downer on the evenin'? Man up princess. This is our life.

SARKO: 'Man up princess'?

DEB: Yeh.

They start cracking up. SARKO starts to get into his bed…

SARKO: 'Man up princess'?!

DEB: Yeh! What? Fuckin' man up!

SARKO: You're a fuckin' dick you are.

DEB: Takes one to know one.

SARKO: Dick.

DEB: Yeh yeh.

SARKO: *(From his bunk.)* So glad I'm stuck with you out here in…You cocked my pillow?! You cocked my fucking pillow?!

DEB: Sweet dreams asshole.

SARKO: You'd better watch your back mate. That's all I'm sayin'. You'd better watch your back.

DEB chuckles to herself.

DEB: Sweet dreams.

SCENE 3

We are back in Chippenham. This time we're in JIM's office which has been converted, badly, from a bedroom.

DEB: Did you literally just move my bed and wardrobe and put your desk in here?

JIM: Pretty much.

DEB: You didn't want to re-decorate or nothin'?

JIM: I only use it for work.

DEB: Thanks by the way. Didn't wait long by the sounds of it.

JIM: Well if you will use your leave to go gallavantin' off on holiday rather than seein' your old man.

DEB: What? Come home and play at happy families?

JIM: Yeh well.

DEB: Go on then give me the info.

JIM: What?

DEB: Your business.

JIM: Oh now, what do you want to know?

DEB: How are you making money from this?

JIM: Simple. Check this out. They use my payment software and every time they use it I get a percentage.

DEB: So you get money for doing nothin' then?

JIM: Well it aint doin' nothin' when I've spent time developin' it is it? But yeh. I aint liftin' a finger once it's out there.

DEB: Thought people could pretty much get it all for free these days anyways? What mugs have you got payin' for it then?

JIM: Mugs who like the harder stuff. Weirder. I don't know.

DEB: Nice. My father, so proud, providin' them paedos with a well run service.

JIM: Shuttup it's not that kind of stuff. Bondage. Hardcore. Bukake.

DEB: Do I want to know what Bukake is?

JIM: Take one Japanese woman and a bunch of Japanese guys and get them to jizz all over her face. Bukake.

DEB: What a nice image. Thanks dad.

JIM: Seriously mate. The stuff that's out there. Caters for all tastes. I aint sayin' I'm a punter but I'm tellin' you now this aint exactly the worst way to earn a livin' if you know what I mean.

DEB: Not your average nine to five.

JIM: You'd love it. Spend my day lookin' at tits and makin' creative decisions about which ones to feature. Fuckin' made mate.

DEB: So it's not just software you're into then?

JIM: Nah, you know me. I figured that if they were making cash from traffic to their sites and using my software to get the money from them why don't I cut out the middle man and make some sites of my own?

DEB: Where do you get your pictures from and that?

JIM: Just rip them from other sites. Easy enough.

DEB: You got it all sewn up aintcha? Fingers in all the pies.

JIM: I wish.

DEB: And you aint got no problem bein' in this business?

JIM: Why should I? Oldest profession in the world.

DEB: Thought that was prostitution?

JIM: Look. They get paid well. There are legislations and that. They choose it. And it is merely providin' a public service. People need to let off steam. Relax. Why, why am I even sayin' all this? Are you some kind of moral police all of a sudden? Do I need to tell you what it is you do for a livin'?

DEB: What? Protect our country?

JIM: Nah – kill people.

DEB: Bit more to it than that.

JIM: Is there? It's all violence at the end of the day. Hurtin' people. Gettin' power over people. We're in the same business mate.

DEB: I fuckin' hope not.

JIM: Do you know what your problem is? You're livin' in a bubble. The life you lead aint real. You're looked after. Fed. Watered. Clothed. Told where to go and what to do. You're not makin' any decisions for yourself. You 'ant no idea what it's like to be a real human being because you're a robot. And you're a miserable robot aren't you Deb? You're not happy. I can tell. And you won't be until you let go and admit you're an animal like the rest of us. Then maybe we can talk.

A pause.

JIM: What?

DEB leaves the room and we transition into the kitchen.

SCENE 4

The kitchen. It's later in the evening of DEB's arrival, after dinner. JO has finished tidying up. JIM is in his office off. DEB is making tea for JO and herself.

DEB: So I'm thinkin' I'll get a job and that. I don't know. Somethin' simple for a while. Settle back.

JO: Good luck!

DEB: Get myself a place, see whether I could live round here again. I don't know.

JO: You don't need a place.

DEB: Reckon it would be good to get back into the old routines.

JO: Thought army was job for life and that?

DEB: Would be nice to have a bit of normality for once.

JO: Careful what you wish for mate.

DEB: Have you seen any of the old lot recently?

JO: No.

DEB: Not out at pub then?

JO: Ant been for a while.

DEB: Fancy goin'?

JO: Now?

DEB: Yeh.

JO: Nah.

DEB: Why not?

JO: Got things to do.

DEB: Got what?

JO: Got a wash on. Got to hang it out. I'm tired anyway.

DEB: You're a barrel of laughs now aintcha?

JO: Yeh well. Aint really been there since. Well, since you were here last. When we were. At that New Year party.

DEB: Oh man.

JO: Dancin' like twats.

DEB: Speak for yourself.

JO: Nickin' vodka from behind the bar.

DEB: Last ones standin' at the lock-in.

JO: Standin'? Don't think so.

DEB: Yeh.

Slight pause.

DEB: Remember summer after your A Levels?

JO: A level. Just the one.

DEB: Right laugh weren't it?

JO: Yeh.

DEB: Down the river with the lads. What happened to Craig then? Ant seen him since school.

JO: Oh blimey. Got some girl from Frome pregnant, got married, got divorced, got a job in Bristol, DJs in some pub out there on thursdays and likes pictures of motorbikes.

DEB: How the fuck do you know all that?

JO: Facebook.

DEB: Oh I see. You don't go to the pub but you make sure you keep up with what everyone's doin'? Like some internet stalker? You're no better than dad.

JO: Piss off I am. And I don't know what pub you're talkin' about because no one goes down the Bell no more. They've all buggered off. All them lot I know what they're doin' now though. Kerry has four kids.

DEB: Four?! What did she do? Grow them in a greenhouse? How did she find time to have four?

JO: Well she was pregnant with her third when you last saw her and she's had another since then. Tone has a job down Co-op in Twerton I think. Lives Foxhill in Bath.

Do you remember Sam-Anne? Moved to fuckin' Jamaica and got herself two mixed-race kids and now speaks with some kind of weird Jamaican patois. All 'Jah bless' this and 'me do this' and 'me do that'. Stupid girl. Constantly on Facebook with her grievances bout boyfriends. Over sharin'. She's a waster.

DEB: Not your best friend then?

JO: Never was.

DEB: So everyone's got their lives sorted then eh?

JO: I don't think you could describe it like that no. I think you're the only one with a proper job.

DEB: What about you then? Don't want a career no more? Year and a half ago you were goin' to be a vet.

JO: With one A Level?

DEB: Alright but you were sayin' workin' down rescue centre and that.

JO: Yeh well don't need to now, eh?

DEB: You doin' alright then?

JO: Yeh.

DEB: Dad treatin' you alright then?

JO: Yeh.

    Pause.

DEB: Look sorry. But. Look. Do you know if. Dad's heard from mum at all?

JO: Don't think so. Maybe. I don't know half of what he's doing in that office.

DEB: Sorry.

JO: No matter. You heard from her?

DEB: Only the once.

JO: Listen, about it all.

DEB: Forget it.

JO: It weren't very. I wasn't. I wanted to at least. Oh bloody hell.

A pause.

DEB: No matter.

A pause.

DEB: Do you know what the best thing out in the desert is?

JO: What's that then?

DEB: A cold shower. Oh man that feels amazin'. End of the day. Not just because of the heat but gettin' all the dust and sand off you. Gettin' the sweat and the caked-on dust off your face. You could almost feel, doin' that, you could almost feel like you're treatin' yourself. Caring for yourself a bit. It was comfort. You know? Somethin' about water. It makes everythin' new again. Clean. Untouched. You know? Oh shuttup Deb. Dickhead.

JO: No don't. I know what you mean.

DEB: Yeh well.

JO: It's like this weather. Aint it? We wait all this time for a fantastic summer and now all I want it to do is rain.

DEB: Yeh I guess.

A Pause.

JO: When your letters would arrive I would take them to the garden to read them on my own.

A Pause. JO isn't looking at DEB. DEB isn't looking at JO.

JO: I'm sorry. I don't know why I said that.

A pause. DEB still can't bring herself to look at JO.

JO: Sorry.

JO gets up and leaves.

SCENE 5

We transition again to the desert.

SARKO: Ah shit mate I'm done.

DEB: Why?

SARKO: Got another letter from Clare.

He hands her the letter and gets into his bunk as she reads it.

DEB: She's a real diamond aint she?

SARKO: I've got myself a class-A psycho there.

He grabs the letter and reads.

SARKO: '…last night I cried for three hours thinking about you.' or '…I can't help but wonder what the other girls there are like – are they fit?', '…whenever I touch myself I try to think of you and your cock but all I ever see is you blown to bits all over the desert.' It's like she wants me to get killed; it would fulfill her fucking fantasies or something.

DEB: She been out with soldiers before?

SARKO: Yeh.

DEB: Yeh.

SARKO has some new lads mags and busies himself with ripping out pages with images of semi-naked women to put on the wall beside his bunk.

SARKO: I got a mate who's on the subs – fuckin' easy life that. The girlfriends and wives have nothing to worry about as no women allowed on board. They lie about, reading and watching DVDs and can't call out so don't even have to speak to them. Fuckin' bliss mate. I'm in the wrong place.

DEB: Is Clare really that worried about you? You have told her I would rather have sex with a turd than go anywhere near you?

SARKO: Oh thanks mate, that's lovely. No. Anyway she thinks lesbians are fakin'. You've got boobs and a fanny. You're a threat.

DEB: Would it help if I spoke to her?

SARKO: Not in any way. She'll think it's some kind of cover up that we've orchestrated. No. I'm going to have to call it a day. Can't take the stress.

DEB: Fair enough.

SARKO: More hassle than they're worth.

DEB: Yeh.

Slight pause. DEB gets some cards out and deals for them to play. Done wordlessly and as if done all the time.

SARKO: You ever had a girlfriend then?

DEB: Nosy twat.

SARKO: I mean it. We've never spoken about it.

DEB: It's none of your business that's why.

SARKO: Why isn't it? You know about my birds.

DEB: Well that's because you've chosen to bore me rigid bout them.

SARKO: Oh sorry didn't realise it was borin'. Thought you were genuinely interested in my life.

DEB: I am. Just not all the fuckin' gory details alright?

SARKO: Why won't you tell me?

DEB: No one's business but mine.

They play on.

SARKO: Do you frig yourself off in your bed then? Or do you use the showers?

DEB: Fucksake! What is wrong with you?

SARKO: I aint had sex for four fuckin' months that's what's wrong with me!

DEB: Get control over yourself, seriously!

SARKO: Yeh but do you?

DEB: No!

SARKO: Not even a little bit?

DEB: What the fuck is a little bit?! Like I'm toying with myself. Being a pussy-tease to myself?!

SARKO: You must do. Seriously. I know you're not a man but you must be feeling it. Do you do it in the shower?

DEB: I am going to zip myself up in my bed in a minute if you don't stop this line of conversation.

SARKO: Yeh but when you do will you then flick yourself to sleep?

DEB: Oh my god!

SARKO: Seriously give me something. Anything.

DEB: What so you can use it as wank ammo?

SARKO: What do you think of when you do it? Celebrities? That bird in Operations? Men?

DEB: Why would I think of men?

SARKO: I don't know. Isn't it like your own version of the 'forbidden'? Like straight women who fantasise about other women? Or men that do the same about men.

DEB: Something you want to tell me Sarko? Got some little secrets of your own have you?

SARKO: No. Shuttup. It was just an example.

DEB: Seems like maybe more than that to me. Tell me what you think about when your beatin' yourself off then. No, I bet I know – it's bondage stuff with figures of authority innit? It's you and the Major tied up in a dungeon and fucking each other free!

SARKO: Shuttup is it. I aint tellin' you what I fantasise about.

DEB: Then why should I tell you about mine?

SARKO: So you admit you have them?

DEB: Of course I do.

SARKO: I fuckin' knew it. And don't be tellin' me you've completely ruled out sex with a man.

DEB: You fuckin' wish. Is this your way of seducin' a woman? No wonder you end up with such psychos.

SARKO: No I'm just sayin' I bet that it's just that you've yet to meet the right one.

DEB: Ah! You're lookin' to convert me. Cure me even. Nice. Good work on the ignorance there mate.

SARKO: I don't believe people are black and white like that/

DEB: /well yeh they are/

SARKO: /not like that, you know what I mean. I think people are just sexual by nature. I don't think you could hand on your heart say that you would never be turned on by a man.

DEB: So with that reasoning you could potentially be turned on by one too then?

SARKO: No that's different.

DEB: What? Why?

SARKO: Because it is. Women need men. For reproduction. It's programmed into your brains. Men just need to do the do. They just need to impregnate. It's just sex to them.

DEB: Any hole's a goal?

SARKO: Exactly.

DEB: Including arseholes belongin' to men?

SARKO: No! Well yes! But not in my case fucksake. You're not listenin'…

DEB: I am and all I'm hearin' is some horny idiot tryin' to argue his way into my knickers.

SARKO: Don't flatter yourself. I only wanted some ammo like you said.

DEB: Well alright I'll give you some.

SARKO: Yeh?

DEB: Yeh, go on then. I will. Here's somethin' to think about when your bashin' your tiny little anaemic bishop.

She pauses for dramatic effect…!

Think about me with the Major, with me watching him skull fuckin' you til you cum all over his shoes.

SARKO: Ok I aint playin' no more.

Gets up to leave.

DEB: Oh you don't like it on the other foot do you? I gave you your ammo, what you complainin' about?

SARKO: You're sick you are.

DEB: I'm sick?

SARKO: Was only tryin' to instigate a conversation.

DEB: Oh hold up a minute mate – let me just get out my tiny violin.

SARKO: See this is what I'm talkin' about.

DEB: Shut up your whining and make me a brew.

She holds up her empty mug.

SARKO: Treat me like your own personal maid you do.

DEB: Go on then.

SARKO: Fuck you.

He grabs the mug and leaves.

DEB: And to you to!

She chuckles to herself alone.

SCENE 6

Back in Chippenham, kitchen. JO is sitting on the countertop looking down at DEB who is clearing up the cards.

JO: If you're stayin' a little while then. Well, there's a new shopping centre opening up in town pretty soon. We could get you kitted out.

DEB: Yeh alright.

JO: Bet you're used to just wearing uniform all the time.

DEB: I had a bag of clothes in my room; where'd they end up?

JO: In the loft. Almost chucked them if I'm honest. Let's sort you out with new stuff yeh?

DEB: What you sayin'?

JO: I'm sayin' if you wear that crap when we go into town you'll be walkin' ten steps behind me like my Muslim wife that's what I'm sayin'.

DEB: I quite like the thought of that.

JO: Don't get no ideas.

DEB: You're smiling.

JO: Course I am. Happy to see you.

DEB: Are you happy the rest of the time though?

JO: Oh don't start. He's your dad. Have some faith.

DEB: Aren't you bothered?

JO: Bothered with what?

DEB: With his work. What he does.

JO: Oh bloody hell. It's just sex Deb.

DEB: But is it love?

JO: Oh well that's deep. What exactly is love mate? Other than
two people needin' each other?

   Pause.

DEB: Love to me feels like cold water on hot skin.

   Pause.

JO: My nan was with gramps for sixty-five years. Sixty-five? I
mean. Surely. Things change.

DEB: I don't know.

JO: There's got to be other stuff that keep you going.
Somewhere to live.

DEB: Spose.

JO: Security.

DEB: Sounds like you've got it sussed.

JO: This aint a bad place to end up.

DEB: You used to say in your letters that you were bored.

JO: I am.

DEB: Don't you want something else then? Some kind of change?

JO: I don't know. No. I don't think so. No.

A really long pause. DEB is working herself up to say something. JO is busying herself.

DEB: When I came back after my first tour. And you were there. I really thought. That what we had. Ah fuck it. I'm shit at this. Fuck it. Just wanted you to know.

A pause.

JO: Alright then. Good. Sorry. Anyways. I'm goin' to bed. You got everything you need?

JO gets up.

DEB: Not really. Have you?

JO doesn't know what to say. She leaves DEB on her own. DEB turns the lights out. Blacks out the room as best she can with the curtains. She sits at the table and lights a cigarette. Somewhere in the distant past SARKO lights a cigarette and watches her.

SCENE 7

DEB is alone in the kitchen with none of the lights on. Above her noises of a television can be heard. The noises sound normal at first but we soon realise that it is porn that is being watched. DEB is listening to this. There are some thumps and then the sound of a bed creaking in rhythm. This goes on for a bit. It stops and there are footsteps, a pause and then the sound of a toilet flushing. A pause and then footsteps of someone coming down the stairs. It is JIM. He enters in his boxers and turns the lights on. He starts at the sight of DEB in the dark.

JIM: If I didn't know better I'd think you had a death wish on me. Sittin' here in the dark you fuckin' vampire. What you doin'?

DEB: Sorry.

JIM: Why aintchoo in bed then?

DEB: Couldn't sleep.

JIM: You get that from me you do. I ant never been much of a sleeper. Used to stay up all night watchin' telly or readin' my comics.

DEB: Comics?

JIM: Yeh! All them superhero ones. Can't go wrong. I was just gettin' some water but I'll have a beer if you will.

DEB: Go on then.

JIM: Thas me girl.

JIM gets them both a beer from the fridge.

DEB: What about Jo?

JIM: She'll be asleep in less than five seconds I'll say. She could sleep through a tornado of pissing sharks she could. Lazy bitch.

DEB: Nice.

JIM: Don't mean it. So. No more desert. No more orders. You must be fuckin' relieved. Just glad you quit before you were blown to bits somewhere in the desert.

DEB: It was just a job to me. I can find another.

JIM: No need to look. Got one right here.

DEB: What? As what? Your chief porn supervisor? Your 'porn buyer'?! No thanks.

JIM: No. As something web based. You could pick up the ropes pretty quick I reckon. Design my sites. Do some administration for the company, that sort of thing. My second in command I suppose. Father and daughter. 'Jim and Daughter' we could call ourselves.

DEB: Give me a break! A father and daughter team that specialise in porn. It sounds like a bad Channel Five documentary.

JIM: It's a job. And I'm offerin' it to you.

DEB: Yeh but it's got to be a job that I actually want to do.

JIM: You sayin' you actually wanted to do the stuff you did out in Afghanistan?

DEB: Sometimes.

JIM: I still don't know where this comes from. You were always a tomboy but I never thought no daughter of mine would be a soldier that's all.

DEB: I was also a peacekeeper.

JIM: And you believe that do you?

DEB: Yeh actually. The people out there are greatful to us.

JIM: Ok.

DEB: We're providin' them with relief. When we have to shoot, then we're talkin' Taliban. The fuckin' evil ones. The bad guys. It's necessary.

JIM: Alright. But what's the point in possessin' a womb if you're also a killer?

DEB: WHAT?! Hold on a minute. Is this about? Is this about me or is this about; wait, what is it about?

JIM: Just don't like it.

DEB: What?

JIM: Somethin' just doesn't quite sit with me.

DEB: About what? Say it.

JIM: You're a woman Deb.

DEB: And there it is! I fuckin' knew it. You're a broken fuckin' record.

JIM: I just don't. It doesn't feel right. In my bones.

DEB: Your poor old bones – so sensitive to change. Will they ever adapt? No they fuckin' won't because they are sitting in the core of a man that thinks that the world is flat and all women are bitches.

JIM: Just talkin' about the facts mate. Men can't cope with it. If you're a bloke and a soldier goes down you have to keep goin'. But how you supposed to do that if it's a woman; cryin' and screamin' in pain? You can't leave her; and then your mission is fucked aint it? And come on mate – mixed barracks? Don't tell me you don't have trouble. You cannot say that on a six-month tour you aint gonna have people shaggin' around, it just aint natural. And it also aint professional. So put that in your pipe and fuckin' smoke it.

DEB: Hold up – male soldiers 'can't cope' with seein' us injured? 'Can't cope'? Oh fuck off. I'm sorry but if we're in a battle situation – which by the way I have been in; I have been shot at and I have shot back. Just because it aint the official line don't mean it don't happen. If we're in a battle situation and the bullets are flyin' round your head and you're runnin' for cover and you see your mate shot down. Regardless of their sex you will do what you can to get them out of harms way, assess their condition, call a medic and then continue on your way. Regardless. And any male soldier that becomes a jibberin' wreck at the sight of a bleedin' woman shouldn't have become a soldier in the first place. And do you know what? I was just as good if not better in that situation than my fellow male soldiers. Because I had to be. And I was carryin' 50 pound of kit in 50 degree heat. Can you do that you fat bastard? Course you can't 'cos you aint trained. But I am. And someone gave me that chance and I took it and I proved that I was capable.

JIM: Sounds like you're tryin' to convince yourself and not me.

DEB: Think what you like.

JIM: What about your periods then?

DEB: What?!

JIM: What do you do if you're in the middle of the battle and you get a period?

DEB: Suddenly I'm really tired.

JO appears in the doorway in her dressing gown.

JO: What's all this noise then?

JIM: Debs is on one of her feminist rants.

JO: Good for her.

JIM: Oh don't you start an all. I'm completely fuckin' outnumbered now in-I? So on that note I'm goin' to go to bed. And I'll leave you two girls to discuss your monthly cycles.

DEB: Yeh yeh.

JIM: Night then.

JIM leaves. JO and DEB sit in the dark together. A short pause. Something passes between them.

DEB: I don't know what I'm even talking about anymore. After everything that's gone on.

JO: He been riling you up has he?

DEB: No.

JO: We got our anniversary comin' up. Your dad's gonna take me to Wookey Hole.

DEB: He's what?

JO: Shuttup I love that place!

DEB: So did I – when I was nine.

JO: Shuttup.

DEB: You're a fuckin' mystery to me.

JO: Well at least I'm something to someone eh?

DEB: What? You see? You say you're ok then you say shit like that. What am I supposed to think?

JO: Sorry.

DEB: Why you sorry?

JO: I don't know. This all just feels like a rubbish welcome home. Burnt bloody lasagna. That's what tonight was. It was a burnt lasagna.

DEB: It don't matter.

JO: I know what'll make it better though.

DEB: What?

A pause. JO smiles at DEB.

DEB: What?

JO: You know what. Ready? Ok then. Gold.

DEB: Oh come on.

JO: Gold.

DEB: Idiot.

JO: No, come on! Gold.

DEB: Fine! Leaf.

JO: Tree.

DEB: Tops.

JO: Bottom.

DEB: Cheeks.

JO: Face.

DEB: Mask.

JO: Hide.

DEB: Under.

JO: Over.

DEB: End.

JO: Finish.

DEB: Stop.

JO: Start.

DEB: Begin.

JO: Again.

DEB: Repeat.

JO: Copy.

DEB: Cat.

JO: Whiskers.

DEB: Beard.

JO: Man

DEB: Woman

JO: Beautiful

DEB: Hair

JO: Brush

DEB: Clean

JO: Tidy

DEB: Up

JO: Down

DEB: There

JO: Here

DEB: You

JO: Me

DEB: I

JO: Lids

DEB: Close

JO: Shut

DEB: Lock

JO: Tight

DEB: Fast

JO: Slow

DEB: Dance

JO: Move

DEB: Out

JO: Reach

DEB: Grab

JO: Take

DEB: Hold

JO: Hug

DEB: Kiss

JO: Touch

DEB: Caress

JO: Kiss

DEB: No repetition!

JO: Why not?

DEB: That's the rules.

JO: Why do we need rules?

A pause.

JO: Kiss.

A pause.

JO: Kiss.

SCENE 8

Afghanistan. Day. The makeshift gym which is an outside affair. DEB and SARKO are lifting weights and spotting for each other. SARKO is lifting at the start.

DEB: Thing is that I heard from her just before when she said she was off to, I don't know, 'find herself' I guess. Greece she said. And now I aint heard from her since and I'm worried she's lost herself instead. And I know that these retreat things can mean she don't have no connection to the outside world, I mean that she won't be on email or nuffin'. And she don't even have a phone and that. And I know I'm being an idiot because I shouldn't expect anythin' else from her. But it was the first, only letter I ever got from her and it wasn't making much sense. And I got this feeling that. Well I thought I'd get more. Or a postcard from Greece or something. I don't know. She said some things about dad and. I don't know.

SARKO stops to catch his breath.

SARKO: Maybe she's joined a cult.

DEB: Thought you were tryin' to make me feel better about this.

SARKO: Just from what you've said about her she sounds like a fuckin' lunatic.

DEB: If I said that about your mum you'd punch my fuckin' head off.

SARKO: Yeh but my mum's an angel. According to you, yours is a 'hippy slut'.

DEB: Fuck you dickhead.

SARKO: Just repeatin' what you said.

DEB: I can say it – she's my mum.

SARKO: Whatever.

DEB: Shuttup and finish your reps.

DEB watches in silence as SARKO completes his set.

DEB: What if it is a commune? Fuck.

SARKO: Look, she's just being a selfish cunt and not tellin' no one where she is. Pretty soon she'll get in touch and then you can have a go at her for being a bitch.

DEB: Yeh and the rest.

SARKO: Your turn. Reduce the weight?

DEB: Piss off.

DEB gets into position and SARKO lowers the weight for her. It is heavy but she is able to do it.

SARKO: You're gettin' better you know?

DEB can't answer and completes her rep. SARKO helps her get the weight on the stand and she breathes heavily.

SARKO: They can say what they like about you; but you can bench with the best of them.

DEB: Is that a compliment Sark? Fuckin' hell.

SARKO: Don't get used to it.

DEB: And what do you mean 'they can say what they like about me'? What do they say?

SARKO: You don't want to know.

DEB: Yeh I do. What do they say?

SARKO: Nothin'! It was a figure of speech you paranoid dick.

DEB: No it wasn't. I know they say shit. What do they say?

SARKO: Why do you care?

DEB: That's my fuckin' decision. Tell me.

SARKO: No. Do your second set.

DEB: No. Tell me.

SARKO: Do your fuckin' set Deb.

DEB: No, fuckin' tell me.

SARKO: They don't say nothin'. I meant it. No one has a problem with you.

DEB: Now you're fuckin' lying.

SARKO: I'm not! You're being a stupid prick. Do your set.

DEB: Well they can all fuck off anyways. I've had enough of the shit I get. Fuck them.

SARKO: What shit? You don't get any shit.

DEB: Yeh I do.

SARKO: Shuttup.

DEB concentrates and does her rep harder and faster than before. She grunts in pain. When she finishes she lets out a yell.

DEB: Show me another fuckin' woman who can do that! Show me one other woman who can fuckin' do that!

SARKO: Easy mate, calm down. You're actin' like you got somethin' to prove.

DEB: Yeh well I have haven't I?

SARKO: Only to yourself.

DEB: Where's my mum Sarko? Where's my fuckin' mum?

SARKO: What is this about? Lower your voice.

DEB: She's disappeared and my dad aint communicatin'. The only person that writes is Jo and she's. She's. I don't fuckin' know what she wants. And why am I here?

SARKO: It's your job you said. Best army in the world you said.

DEB: But why am I here? No one wants me here.

SARKO: Oh come on dickhead.

DEB: I'm serious. I put my life into this place.

SARKO: Get over yourself mate. You aint so special. We all feel like that.

DEB: Then what's the fuckin' point?

SARKO: I'm the fuckin' point. The lads are the fuckin' point. We can all be each other's point. Whatever and that. Whatever. Shuttup. What's wrong with you?

DEB: I'm not cryin'.

SARKO: Yeh you are.

DEB: What the fuck is goin' on? Where is she?

SARKO: Pissin' about in the sunshine. What do you care? Thought you hated her? Thought she was a psycho?

DEB: Yeh.

SARKO: Anyways. This is home for us aint it?

DEB: This place is fuckin' scary Sark.

SARKO: Of course it is.

DEB: You always looks so together. You always look like you're in your element.

SARKO: So do you.

DEB: Do I? Don't feel it.

SARKO: You aint special Deb. Everyone feels like that.

DEB: I just need somethin' that. I. Comfort. I'm fuckin' soft in- I? Fuckin' pussy that's what I am.

Before she can protest SARKO kisses her. He holds her so she can't pull away and she struggles then lets it happen. When he stops and moves away she punches him in the face incredibly hard. He recoils holding his bleeding face.

DEB: Prick!

DEB is crying now. She can't stop herself.

DEB: That's not what I meant. That's not what I fuckin' meant.

She runs off.

SCENE 9

Chippenham. The kitchen again with JO and DEB.

JO: It's so nice havin' you around again. I wish you felt like you could relax.

DEB: I'm just watchin' you and you don't seem the same no more. Sound stupid but you've almost changed shape.

JO: Look. You're worryin'. Your dad's a lovely bloke.

DEB: No he aint.

JO: He is. He looks after me.

DEB: Does he?

JO: He provides for me.

DEB: Barely.

JO: I don't know what you've dreamt up.

DEB: I know him is all.

JO: And I know how to handle him.

A pause.

DEB: When I was out there I would have to search the women. On patrol. I would do this and I never once found anything other than what you'd expect. A body. Arms. Legs. Breasts. Under all that fabric. It got me wonderin' about them as bodies. 'Cos they're so covered up but underneath. I mean. What kind of sex must they have with their husbands?

JO: You're interested in everyone's business aren't you?

DEB: Like. I'm looking at this woman and thinkin' it must be pretty shit livin' under all that cloth all the time. I'm thinkin' her husband must be keepin' her under lock and key. That their sex must be horrible. But have I got it wrong? Is it actually really fuckin' sensual? When they're home and behind the bedroom door. Do you think she lets him undress her really slowly? Releasing her hair, her face, her skin? Does he drink in every part of her before kissing her all over? Knowing that he's the only one on this earth who is doing that. Right there. In that moment. The two of them. Or am I assumin' right? Is is cold, mechanical, brutal?

JO: Well I guess you'll never know.

DEB: Sometimes what you see can be misleadin'.

JO: Yes, what?

DEB: Tell me what I'm seeing is misleadin'.

JO: He's your dad Deb, why you bein' like this?

DEB: What's he like in bed?

JO: Shuttup!

DEB: Is he gentle?

JO: Stop it.

DEB: Kind? Lovin'? Generous?

JO: Stop.

DEB: Does he make sure you cum first? Does he kiss you? Does he get you ready before he goes in?

JO: Deb…

DEB: Or does he just take it? Does he make you suck it? Does he watch the nasty ass porn while he's fuckin' you from behind.

JO: I don't mind though.

DEB: Really?

JO: No. I don't. In fact. Sometimes I actually like it. Oh aint that a shocker. 'Woman likes porn' I can see the headlines now. Gets me goin' sometimes.

DEB: Alright then…

JO: I find this bloody filthy woman inside me who wants to do all sorts of things, and I like it. It's that buzz. It's fun. It's a fantasy. It's somethin' to look forward to in my day when I get to let go and do as I'm told. Not everythin' is fairy lights and scented flippin' candles. I don't want a cuddle, I want to be fucked. Oh you don't like that do you? Suddenly regrettin' askin' are you? Sorry I aint perfect. Sorry I aint pure. And it's nothin' to be ashamed of anyways. I know what I like.

The distinction between Chippenham and Afghanistan gets blurred from here. SARKO and JIM and JO appear in both.

SARKO: I wanted to talk to you. Why you been avoidin' me? I should be the one...punching me in the fuckin' face?

DEB doesn't respond.

SARKO: Look I am sorry. I am. Last thing I want to do is piss you off. Say something please.

DEB: It's ok.

SARKO: But it's not though is it? You're angry. Look. I guess. Look. I got carried away. I thought you wanted it because you and me, we're. Well we're different aint we? I can talk to you. I appreciate that. It makes sense you know? I like what we've got.

DEB: What have we got?

SARKO: Well you know. It's easy aint it? You let me talk, you understand me. And, you know, I protect ya.

DEB: You what?

SARKO: Keep an eye on things for ya. It's difficult out here and that. I don't mind. I don't mind lookin' after ya.

DEB: Is that what you think you're doing?

SARKO: Well yeh Deb. It's obvious aint it? How else would you have kept the other lads off your back? They know to stay away because you're with me. They know you're my girl.

A shift.

DEB: The thing is, I don't like it. I'm sorry I just don't. And I don't like you talkin' to me bout it alright? I have no interest in it. In fact I think it's horrible. And just because you think you're some kind of enlightened human bein' to be so liberal about it all don't mean that I have to.

JIM: It's just sex.

DEB: I'm sorry, you can justify it as much as you like but I don't like it. And I'm guessin' neither did mum.

JIM: What's she got to do with it?

DEB: You tell me.

JIM: Look your mum had issues. She was messed up way before I got to her. We weren't right together. I know it's hard to hear but she wasn't a good person.

DEB: What is a good person then?

JIM: Well now. There's a question.

Another shift.

SARKO: Why you lookin' at me like that?

DEB: Where did you get all this from? We're mates. I aint your 'girl'.

SARKO: You know what I mean.

DEB: No I don't. I don't need nobody lookin' out for me.

SARKO: I thought I was doing you a favour. You're takin' this all wrong. I mean fair play you've done well out here but all I'm sayin' is that I've been on my guard. For you.

DEB: You're fuckin' delusional.

SARKO: Look whatever. You can't say that you haven't noticed. Us. Noticed. Things.

DEB: Who the hell do you think you are?

SARKO: What?

DEB: All my life I've been able to look after myself so why the fuck would I need you now? I can't believe you got me so wrong.

SARKO: I'm sorry Deb but I don't think you're being honest with yourself.

DEB: What? I've done nothing but work my arse off to prove myself to you fucking pricks and you still think I need protecting? I knew you were a stupid cunt but I didn't realise you were this bad. And by the way even if I was interested in men; why the fuck would I want you?

Another shift.

JIM: Your mum would leave you in your room, lock the door and go down the pub. I don't know why you've got this obsession with her. She was a fuckin' awful mother. Don't you remember what it was like? She was a depressive. She was this massive cloud hangin' around. I tried everythin'.

DEB: Like what?

JIM: Well I dunno. She was hard to live with. You must remember. It weren't all me you know. You were just as bad with her.

DEB: Yeh I know.

JIM: I don't know why you're pinnin' so much on her. She's gone Deb. She's a waster. She's not worth it.

Pause.

DEB: Why did she get so depressed?

JIM: Well I don't fuckin' know do I? She was a nutjob Deb! Why does anyone go mad?

DEB: She weren't mad. No she weren't. She was lost. I remember the arguments. I remember the bitchin'. The insults. I remember her bangin' around the kitchen in tears. I remember you in the telly room, smokin' and ignorin' her. I remember you just not sayin' anythin', walkin' past her in the hallway when she was slumped on the stairs, unable to move herself because she was so fuckin' sad. I learnt stuff from you, you know? I learnt that this was all normal. That when mum was like this you just leave her be. Let her blow off steam. Let it pass. I ignored her like you. But really what we should have done. What you should have done dad. Was take her in your arms and hold onto her as tight as you could. That's what you should have done. So why didn't you?

JIM: When you came along it was like her light switched off for good.

DEB: What?

JIM: She may have had some kind of mad in her from the start mate, but as soon as you appeared; she'd gone.

A shift.

JO: Look at your face. It's like I'm openin' up a whole new world for you. But don't get me wrong. I don't like the fake stuff. The professionals with their tits and no hair. It's all just so, I don't know, clean. And sex aint clean is it? It's filthy. It's sweaty and smelly and sticky. It's awkward. And uncomfortable. And sometimes a bit humiliatin'. And I like that. So when I'm watching I like it when it's more real. Like, real people's sex. On 'youporn' or whatever. Real couples and that. We're lookin' in on them and seein' all the things they're up to. All the nasty, weird things. In their bedrooms, in their cars, in their kitchens. Their strange bodies, their noises, fumblings, twisting, fucking. And actually it's really quite hot. I like it.

DEB: So you'd do it would you? Put yourself up there?

JO: Course I would. I have.

DEB: What?

JO: Well, Jim did.

DEB: What are you talking about?

JO: Jim put one up.

DEB: He did what?

JO: He put it on. He put it. He put it online.

DEB: …

JO: It's fine.

DEB: What is it of?

JO: Of us. You know.

DEB: …

JO: But it's ok. I don't mind

DEB: …

JO: I don't. It's funny. It was night vision so my face looks like one of them zombie faces in a movie or somethin'. I didn't even know he was filming.

DEB: …

JO: And my fat arse.

DEB: …

JO: And it's not even that long. It's only about a minute or two. And it's not all that interestin'. Just my bum. And his. Can't see him actually. Just me. And my zombie face. All these thousands of people lookin' from god knows where around the world. At my bum. Those thousands of people.

DEB: …

JO: Oh god.

DEB: …

JO: But. It's ok anyways, because you wouldn't know it was me. You can't tell that it's me.

DEB: Is it still on there?

JO: Yes. But he said he wouldn't do it again.

DEB: How do you know he won't?

JO: Well I don't do I? I just have to trust him.

DEB: Why you pretendin' to me? Why you pretendin' everythin' is ok?

JO: I'm not.

DEB: You are. It's fuckin' killin' me. Stop it. You're shakin'.

JO: I can't

JO breaks down.

A shift.

SARKO: I got a theory about you.

DEB: Oh here we go…

SARKO: You keep everythin' so close to your chest. You hide as much as you can. But really I don't think that there's anythin' there. I don't think you're hidin' anythin'. It's all about the mystique. You create an air of mystery and people think you're more interestin' than you are. Just because you appear to have secrets don't mean your secrets are all that interestin'.

DEB: You're talkin' out of your fat arse.

SARKO: No I aint. I know a million women like you. You keep us guessin' because the truth is so mundane. All the prick teases down the pub makin' out like they're so fuckin' special. Only givin' over titbits of information. Suggestively lookin' at you when they've said somethin' that could mean somethin' else. It's all a fuckin' game to you lot aint it? It's all just about drivin' us mad with fuckin' lust and then expectin' us to just take a deep breath and walk away.

DEB: You've got a very high opinion of yourself haven't you?

SARKO: Fuck off do I. I'm just sayin' I think you're nothin' but hot air. And I don't believe a word of it; you've had girlfriends? Fuck off. You're so poppin' for it you couldn't be more obvious if you tried. You're kiddin' yourself Deb. I think you're all talk and actually. Actually you're a fuckin' lesbo virgin and what you really need is a damn good screw.

A shift.

JIM: What happens between a man and wife is their business.

DEB: Not when it's clear that what's goin' on aint makin' them happy no more. You proud of your work are you? You really proud of what you do?

JIM: Oh come on Deb. You've seen it. You've seen how dark it is out there. I'm on the surface of it. Not even scratchin' it. I'm the tip of the flippin' iceberg what's gonna send us right down into the pits of hell/

DEB: /dramatic/

JIM: /There are people out there with things in their head that you don't even want to glimpse. The majority of people have thoughts every fuckin' day that, if they ever acted on them, you'd be yellin' for the return of capital fuckin' punishment. Don't you tell me you've never wanted to really hurt someone? Attack someone? Come on! Course you have! You're a soldier; you're programmed to think these things. But what if it don't stop there? Suddenly your punching someone. Choking someone. Cuttin' someone. It aint such a leap to the nastier stuff then. Is it? We like the base, the dirty, the wrong. We fuckin' lust after it every waking hour. So why, when we're all thinkin' it, can't we indulge in it? Just a bit? Just to relax? Not hurtin' no one. Just a man and his computer.

DEB: But it aint though is it? It aint. Sometimes it aint just a computer.

JIM: Well that aint my problem is it? All I'm sayin' is that we can't go against our nature. Why deny what we really are?

DEB: I think dad. That sometimes you think I'm your son. I think that sometimes you forget I'm a woman.

A shift.

SARKO: I reckon you're a virgin in both senses. Completely unexplored. Aint that true?

DEB: You better take that back. Who the fuck…?

SARKO: Just tryin' to instigate a debate darlin'. You like debates I thought. Why aint you playin' along?

A shift.

JIM: And when you're dealin' with psychos then there's no boundaries as far as I'm concerned. Your mother was a waster. She had no direction. She gave me shit most days. It wore me down. What's the point in havin' a wife if you can't have it on tap whenever you want it?

A shift.

SARKO: What's the point in havin' you out here if there's not goin' to be no perks?

A shift.

DEB: And I felt like I was floating somewhere between a massive bottomless pit and a huge gaping black hole. There was no light anywhere. Anywhere. No light at all. And do you know what I did? I shut my eyes and I thought of you.

A shift.

SARKO uses his strength to overpower DEB. They struggle. He pushes her down facing away from him and holds her head on the floor with his hand. He pulls her trousers and knickers down and fucks her aggressively from behind. DEB doesn't make a sound. JO and JIM watch impassively. DEB's eyes are screwed up shut. When SARKO has finished he doesn't pull DEB's trousers up but instead does his own trousers up and leaves. JIM leaves also. DEB, still seated, pulls her trousers up then moves slowly to the wall. Reaching up she hits a button and a shower is activated. She sits huddled as the water comes down and lets it soak her.

SCENE 10

JO: You were always quietly watchin' everythin'. Always on the edge of the group. Chucklin' at the jokes, never sayin' much though. Big sunny days by the river. Smokin'. Drinkin'. Backies on the bikes. Huddled together round a disposable BBQ trying to cook bacon. Swimmin' in our knickers and t-shirts. And you. There on the sidelines watchin'. Not quite confident enough to join in proper. But we didn't mind you 'cos you would always bring crisps wouldn't you? And booze from your dad's cupboard. And you'd always laugh at my jokes. You were a kid I suppose but so were we. And you never really seemed to mind that you were different. Your big green eyes. I remember Craig noticed and would joke that he'd have to have a word with you 'eyein' up his bird'.

DEB: I didn't know I was that obvious.

JO: Pining.

DEB: Sorry.

JO: Don't be. You know your letters you left for us? Ones we weren't supposed to open unless.

DEB: You opened yours didn't you?

JO: Yeh. Sorry.

DEB: Don't matter now anyway.

JO: Thank you. For those things you wrote.

DEB: Don't matter.

JO: Yeh it does. You promise you're not going back?

DEB: Yeh.

JO: Good.

DEB: I don't have nothin' there no more. I thought it was my family but it aint.

JO: We're your family Deb.

DEB: Not really.

JO: I wish I was.

DEB: Come with me.

JO: Where?

DEB: I don't know.

JO: I can't.

DEB: She said I was to. Come with her. I was to find her. I was to. And I thought 'Fuck you'. I thought 'why would I do that?'. Fucking psycho. But. She. Isn't. She's this woman. Who is who I. Need. Jo. I. Oh. I need her. So badly. Oh god I don't know where she is. And she thinks I hate her. And I don't. Oh god I don't. And she's nowhere. And someone has ripped out everything inside me. I feel ripped clean. Ripped empty. And she can't want me. Why would she want me? She won't want me.

JO: She was fightin' for you, you know?

DEB: What?

JO: That night in the pub. When she heard about me and your dad. She came in when I was workin' and she dragged me off a stool. She went at me. And I didn't stop her. Because I knew she was right. But Deb, she didn't come for me because of your dad. It was because of you. She was angry with me because I'd done this to you.

DEB: What?

JO: I promise. It's completely the truth. She was fighting for you.

DEB: Come with me.

JO: No.

DEB: Come with me.

JO leaves. DEB is alone.

DEB: When you go out you get your kit and they take your photo. We call them the 'death photos' because they're the ones they will use to send to the press when you're injured or killed. In my last tour they took the photo and I was blinkin'. Fucksake. They were in a rush so they wouldn't let me do another and they were all like 'better make doubly sure you don't get killed then hadn't you?'. It really fucked me off. Because I knew that if I did then I would definitely have my stupid blinkin' photo in every bloody newspaper and then that would be it. That would be the only way people remember me. Because even if there has been multiple deaths you will always get a photo of the female soldier because that's interestin' to folk. That's what sells papers aint it?

Anyway. So yeh. They take your photos. But before that what you do is write your letters. To be opened by your loved ones in the event of your death. Man that was hard. Writin' them. What do you say? With dad's I just basically said a load of mundane shit about lovin' him and 'despite the ups and downs' etcetera. With Jo I told her how I felt and what a wonderful woman I think she is. But with mum. Well for a start it was all a bit bloody academic because we didn't have an address for her so actually I still got the letter with me. But I wanted to still write it. And I said. Well.

She gets the letter out and reads.

Ok. All the usual stuff about missin' her and that. That I love her no matter what. But.

She reads for a moment.

What I didn't write. And what I should have. Was. That I think that she has this, like, massive huge heart inside her and that no one's let her use it properly. And that I'm sorry for not. For not standin' up for her more.

She puts the letter back in her pocket.

I've been covered in this thin film of dust see? Not just in the desert. I've felt like my skin hasn't been able to breath.

DEB holds her face up to the sun, breathes in and smiles. Lights fade to black. End.

WWW.OBERONBOOKS.COM